Lincoln Stories for Leaders

LINCOLN STORIES FOR LEADERS

by
Donald T. Phillips

THE SUMMIT PUBLISHING GROUP

THE SUMMIT PUBLISHING GROUP
One Arlington Centre, 1112 East Copeland Road, Fifth Floor
Arlington, Texas 76011
summit@dfw.net
www.summitbooks.com

Printed in the United States of America

01 00 99 98 97   010   5 4 3 2 1

Library of Congress Cataloging-in-Publication Data

   Lincoln, Abraham, 1809-1865.
      Lincoln stories for leaders / [compiled] by Donald T. Phillips.
         p. cm.
      ISBN 1-56530-242-7
      1. Lincoln, Abraham, 1809-1865--Anecdotes. 2. Lincoln,
   Abraham, 1809-1865--Humor. 3. Leadership--Anecdotes. I.
   Phillips, Donald T. (Donald Thomas), 1952- . II. Title.
   E457.99.L495 1997
   973.7'092--dc21   96-51265
                                                          CIP

Cover design by Dennis Davidson
Book design by John Baird

CONTENTS

PREFACE

Ever since the publication of my first book, people have consistently asked me about Abraham Lincoln's stories and anecdotes—what those stories were, why he told them, and how they may be used by leaders today. I hope this book, *Lincoln Stories for Leaders*, fulfills those many requests and, in so doing, becomes an interesting companion volume to *Lincoln on Leadership*.

Abraham Lincoln was one of the world's great storytellers. Having been raised on the Bible, from which he learned to read, Lincoln took his cue from Jesus Christ, who told parables to convey a profound message to others. As president of the United States, Lincoln did the same. To people with whom Lincoln came in contact, it was the stories they remembered most about him. And, as president, Lincoln spun a yarn or two for nearly everyone he encountered.

Hundreds of these stories still exist, having been passed down through the years in old books that simply state one anecdote and then move on to another. Newer books about Lincoln's "wit and wisdom" often add the circumstances under which the stories were told. But Lincoln's humor, along with the symbols and imagery he employed, remains largely unstudied and misunderstood. While Lincoln's wit was spontaneous, his telling of stories and anecdotes was anything but unplanned. During years of reading and researching Lincoln's writings and sayings, I observed that his stories could very easily be cataloged under various headings that reveal much of the man's personality and exceptional understanding of people—not to mention his leadership style and philosophy.

The arrangement of stories in this book is my perception of what Lincoln contained in his head. And, faster than a computer, he could pull out just the right one to get across his message to clinch an argument or to shed light on the truth.

Lincoln's stories can be employed in everyday situations. They are for practical usage, and they are for leaders in all walks of life who wish to interact more gracefully with their people. They also are testament to the fact that after more than six score and seven years—Lincoln speaks to us still.

INTRODUCTION

Abraham Lincoln has come to be regarded as the only president of the United States who was a true humorist—in the tradition of Mark Twain or Will Rogers. But he was more than that—much more. He was a true craftsman in the art of storytelling and a master of skilled conversation. Lincoln could talk to anyone. He had a rustic upbringing that enabled him to chat with a simple backwoods farmer, the intellectual capacity to hold his own with a brilliant scientist, and the political savvy to get the best of any seasoned politician. And Lincoln not only possessed a terrific sense of humor, he also had the great virtue of being able to laugh at himself.

During an address delivered to a group of newspaper editors in Bloomington, Indiana, Lincoln began by stating that he lacked the credentials to speak to such a distinguished group. He said he felt much like he did back when he was riding the circuit in Illinois and happened to pass a woman on horseback. As he turned out to let her by, she gazed intently at him and said: "I do believe you are the ugliest man I ever saw!" "Madam," he replied, "I expect you're right, but I just can't help it." "No," she said, "you can't help it. But you might stay at home."

Storytelling came naturally to Lincoln. He inherited the ability partly from his father, Thomas Lincoln, who was a popular yarn-spinner of his day. Later in life, after a long day's work as a lawyer riding the circuit in Illinois, Abraham would pass the time with his colleagues at the local tavern where each would take turns telling a favorite anecdote. Nearly every night, for six months out of every year, they would hold storytelling contests in front of standing-room-only crowds eager to be amused and entertained. Over the years, as one can imagine, Lincoln not only built up a good supply of tales, he also honed his craft and perfected his skill at relating them.

Lincoln's humor was a major component of his ability to persuade people. He knew the effect it had and used it to the utmost. Oddly enough, it also aided him politically by becoming an obsession with the public. The stories made him a folk hero in his own time. People became fascinated with his quick wit and hilarious yarns, and, as a result, many of his humorous anecdotes found their way into print while he was still alive. There were, in fact, literally hundreds of stories attributed to Lincoln that the president himself had never heard.

During those years in the White House, his storytelling became so legendary that amusing tales started to circulate about *him*. One that he was fond of telling on himself was about two Quaker women in a railway coach who were overheard in a conversation:

"I think Jefferson will succeed," said the first.

"Why does thee think so?" asked the second.

"Because Jefferson is a praying man."

"And so is Abraham a praying man."

"Yes, but the Lord will think Abraham is joking."

Carl Schurz, a Republican contemporary of Lincoln, and later a Union general, recounted his first meeting with the future president:

> All at once, after the train had left a way station, I observed a great commotion among my fellow passengers, many of whom jumped from their seats and pressed eagerly around a tall man who had just entered the car. They addressed him in the most familiar style: "Hello,

Abe! How are you?" and so on. And he responded in the same manner: "Good evening, Ben! How are you, Joe? Glad to see you, Dick!" And there was much laughter at some things he said, which, in the confusion of voices, I could not understand. "Why," exclaimed my companion, the committee man, "there's Lincoln, himself!" He pressed through the crowd and introduced me to Abraham Lincoln, whom I then saw for the first time...He received me with an offhand cordiality, like an old acquaintance...and we sat down together. In a somewhat high-pitched but pleasant voice... [he] talked in so simple and familiar a strain, and his manner and homely phrase were so absolutely free from any semblance of self-consciousness or pretension of superiority, that I soon felt as if I had known him all my life, and we had very long been close friends. He interspersed our conversations with all sorts of quaint stories, each of which had a witty point applicable to the subject in hand and not seldom concluded an argument in such a manner that nothing more was to be said.

Carl Schurz was not the only person who heard Abraham Lincoln tell a story. As a matter of fact, nearly *everyone* who came in contact with the future sixteenth president heard him relate some kind of yarn. Storytelling had become a natural ingredient in his personal conversation. And because of years of hearing and telling them, Lincoln possessed an overwhelming inventory of anecdotes, jokes, and stories—any one of which he could instantly employ for just the right situation. Lincoln had become a master at the art of storytelling, and he used that ability purposefully and effectively when he became president of the United States.

Part of the craft of storytelling rests in its apparent artlessness. When a person tells a story during the course of normal conversation, he is generally not perceived as much of an intellectual. However, it requires just as much intelligence, if not more, to skillfully weave an appropriate anecdote into a conversation as it does to studiously argue a point with facts and figures.

Clearly, Lincoln thought a great deal about his craft and definitely developed a strategy in employing stories effectively. "I believe I have the popular reputation of being a storyteller," Lincoln once said as president, "but I do not deserve the name in its general sense, for it is not the story itself, but its purpose, or effect, that interests me. I often avoid a long and useless discussion by others or a laborious explanation on my own part by a short story that illustrates my point of view. So, too, the sharpness of a refusal or the edge of a rebuke may be blunted by an appropriate story, so as to save wounded feelings and yet serve the purpose. No, I am not simply a storyteller, but storytelling as an emollient saves me much friction and distress. I do not seek applause nor to amuse people—I want to convince them."

Lincoln cultivated his precision storytelling into a formidable political weapon. "If you have an audience who has the time and is inclined to listen, lengthen it out slowly as if from a jug," he advised. "If you have a poor listener, hasten it, shorten it, shoot it out of a popgun." During the Lincoln-Douglas debates of 1858, Stephen A. Douglas actually feared this skill possessed by his opponent. "Every one of his stories seems like a whack upon my back," said Douglas. "Nothing else, not any of his arguments or any of his replies to my questions, disturbs me. But when he begins to tell a story, I feel that I am to be overmatched."

And most who came into contact with Lincoln while he was president found themselves overmatched. One-on-one, Lincoln could convince anybody of just about anything. Even the brightest leading citizens of the era were dominated by Lincoln during a personal exchange. Many who called on him at the White House to obtain some favor found themselves in the hall wondering how Lincoln got rid of them. Thurlow Weed, a prominent journalist and political organizer, once sat down after a meeting with him and wrote a letter to Lincoln that stated, in part: "I do not, when with you, say half I intend, partly because I do not like to 'crank,' and partly because you talk me out of my convictions and apprehensions. So bear with me, please, now, till I free my mind." In turn, Lincoln once wrote to Weed: "I am sure if we could meet we would not part with any unpleasant impression on either side."

President Lincoln also turned to humor to help alleviate the strain of his office and the impact that the loss of life during the Civil War had on him. Laughter gave him a momentary break from his troubles. "I tell you the truth," he once related to a friend, "when I say that a funny story, if it has the element of genuine wit, has the same effect on me that I suppose a good square drink of whiskey has on an old drunk; it puts new life into me. The fact is I have always believed that a good laugh was good for both the mental and the physical digestion."

When a visitor once commented on how tired the president appeared, Lincoln replied that "his earbones ached" for a good story because he had pretty much exhausted his own supply of yarns "that were good to cheer up people in this hard world." Lincoln said that he had been "giving out so much cheer to the generals and congressmen" that he had "pumped himself dry and must take in a new supply from some source at once." So we can see that Lincoln not only used the stories to cheer himself up but also to elevate the confidence of those around him.

Even in the most serious moments with his cabinet members, though, Lincoln would take the time to tell an anecdote and illustrate to his subordinates exactly how he felt. Often, if they were discussing policy or a certain direction the country should take, the president's story would end the conversation. Other times he merely related the tale for amusement. A case in point occurred when Lincoln first showed his cabinet the original draft of the Emancipation Proclamation. After he had finished reading, one cabinet member was bold enough to break the silence with a few suggested changes and then, eventually, all the members had their shot at his document.

"Gentlemen," said Lincoln, "this reminds me of the story of the man who had been away from home, and when he was coming back was met by one of his farmhands, who greeted him after this fashion: 'Sir, the little pigs are dead, and the old sow's dead, too, but I didn't like to tell you all at once.'"

Lincoln primarily used his skill in telling stories to persuade others. As one of his former law apprentices related it, he communicated stories now largely "for business, to give a hint or enforce an argument." This was a skill possessed by Lincoln that he used to his utmost advantage as a leader. "They say I tell a great many stories," he said. "I reckon I do; but I have learned from long experience that *plain* people take them as they run—[and] are more easily *influenced* through the medium of a *broad* and humorous illustration than in any other way."

Lincoln once attempted to convince his argumentative secretary of the treasury, Salmon P. Chase, that it was a good idea for the government to issue interest-bearing paper currency as a means of raising money to support the war effort. Chase, however, objected to the proposal and argued that it was unconstitutional. Rather than simply ordering Chase to do it, which he could have as president, Lincoln chose to tell him the story of a sea captain who ran his vessel on a rock and knocked a hole in her bottom. He set his men to pumping, and he went to pray before a figure of the Virgin Mary in the bow of the ship. But the leak gained on them. It looked at last as if the vessel would go down with all on board. The captain, at length, in a fit of rage at not having his prayers answered, seized the figure of the Virgin and threw it overboard. Suddenly, the leak stopped, the water was pumped out, and the vessel got safely to port. When docked for repairs the statue of the Virgin Mary was found stuck head foremost in the hole.

But Chase, not understanding the point of the story, essentially said: "I don't see your point, Mr. President."

"Why, Chase," responded Lincoln, "I don't intend precisely to throw the Virgin Mary overboard, and by that I mean the Constitution, but I'll stick it in the hole if I can. These rebels are violating the Constitution in order to destroy the Union. I will violate the Constitution, if necessary, to save the Union; and I suspect, Chase, that our Constitution is going to have a rough time of it before we get done with this fight."

And Chase finally responded that he now understood and would go ahead with the idea—and that the president would "never hear another negative word about it from me."

The beauty of this story is that Lincoln told it in the first place. He didn't have to tell it. He could have argued with Chase for hours until he was blue in the face. No amount of reasoning could have persuaded him. And he could have ordered him to proceed—which Chase would have done halfheartedly and begrudgingly. But Lincoln, in less than five minutes (really, the time it took to tell the story), prevailed upon him to do the job on his own—willingly and enthusiastically.

Stories, like pictures, speak a thousand words. What's more, recent research in the field of leadership confirms Lincoln's strategy and emphasizes the role of stories as powerful motivational tools that spread loyalty, commitment, and enthusiasm.

As a communicator, Abraham Lincoln also liberally utilized colloquial expressions with symbols and imagery for the express purpose of influencing and persuading his audience. His "down-home" figures of speech attracted people, kept their attention, and, in many cases, endeared people to him. These quaint expressions were an important part of his image as a common man—and he used them so frequently that they must have been genuine. Lincoln could compare Horace Greeley to "an old shoe—good for nothing…and so rotten that nothing can be done with him," or Salmon P. Chase to a "bluebottle fly, laying his eggs in every rotten spot he can find," and then turn around and tell others that "I don't amount to pig tracks in the War Department."

Lincoln's colloquialisms could also be biting and to the point—especially when discussing his procrastinating generals. When told that General George Meade was from Pennsylvania, where the next crucial battle was about to be fought, Lincoln replied that his new commander would "fight well on his own dunghill." But, after the victory at Gettysburg, when Meade only followed the defeated army of Robert E. Lee as the Confederates escaped back into Virginia, the president told Meade personally that the general reminded him of "an old woman trying to shoo her geese across a creek."

After his disastrous loss at Chicamauga Creek, General William Rosecrans was described by the president as "confused and stunned like a duck hit on the head." George McClellan had "the slows," and the Army of the Potomac was "McClellan's bodyguard." If the general didn't fight soon, said Lincoln, "both he and I will be in a bad row of stumps."

And later in the war, when new commanding general Ulysses S. Grant unveiled to the president his grand plan to involve all the armies of the Union in a centralized attack against the Confederacy, Lincoln cheerfully responded that "those not skinning can hold a leg."

Discerning Abraham Lincoln's humor through his stories, anecdotes, and earthy figures of speech is a key to understanding not only his personality but his leadership style as well. Lincoln had a story for illustrating each attribute that a leader must possess. He justified compassion, consistency, and flexibility with appropriate stories—each applied under differing circumstances and varying situations. In one moment he could explain the dangers of wasting time and in the next the wisdom of a patient and calculating approach. Lincoln also possessed an unusually large and diverse number of stories that he would use to justify his decisive actions and illustrate the value of planning and vision.

Most of these stories were related in personal conversations—one-on-one with followers. Lincoln realized that chatting informally with one or two people allows a leader to pick up the more subtle nuances of how people actually feel and think. Informal gatherings not only build trust, respect, and fellowship but also give people the opportunity to express their true feelings. And *the truth* is something that all leaders need to hear. Additionally, *loyalty* is more often won through such personal contact than in any other way.

Abraham Lincoln understood what all leaders must understand if they are to be effective; that is, *persuasion* and *inspiration*, rather than coercion or dictatorship, show respect for the dignity and the rights of the individual. And one of the best ways to persuade and inspire people is with a simple, unassuming story.

As well as being an active process, leadership is very much symbolic. It involves the mobilization and motivation of followers who were previously unmoved. As a result, leaders must appeal to emotions as well as to intellect. They must lift people up to a higher level of awareness, commitment, and motivation. Stories are a proper and effective tool for doing so. In addition, if employed well, they can move people swiftly—and in large numbers. Because they appeal to the emotions, stories and anecdotes can be extraordinarily important during times of great crisis or great change. Abraham Lincoln's strategic employment of these wondrous weapons during the Civil War makes his achievements as a leader all the more remarkable.

PART
I

Lincoln Stories
for
General Leadership

COMPASSION

Toward the end of the Civil War, Lincoln was constantly pressured to enact some measure of revenge on the Confederacy and "hang the traitors." But he would have none of it and preferred to treat them all the same way he treated those he whipped while wrestling in his youth. Lincoln would "let 'em up easy." When General William Tecumseh Sherman explicitly asked the president whether he wanted Jefferson Davis captured or allowed to escape, this was the reply:

"I'll tell you, General," replied Lincoln, "what I think of taking Jeff Davis. Out in Sangamon County there was an old temperance lecturer who was very strict in the doctrine and practice of total abstinence. One day, after a long ride in the hot sun, he stopped at the house of a friend, who proposed making him a lemonade. As the mild beverage was being mixed, the friend insinuatingly asked if he wouldn't like a drop of something stronger to brace up his nerves after the exhausting heat and exercise. 'No,' replied the lecturer, 'I couldn't think of it; I'm opposed to it on principle'; but, he added with a longing glance at the black bottle that stood conveniently at hand, 'if you could manage to put in a drop unbeknownst to me, I guess it wouldn't hurt me much.' Now, General, Mr. Lincoln concluded, I am bound to oppose the escape of Jeff Davis; but if you could manage to let him slip out unbeknownst-like, I guess it wouldn't hurt me much."

"And that," General Sherman later remarked, "is all I could get out of the government as to what its policy was concerning the rebel leaders until Stanton assailed me for Davis's escape."

CONSISTENCY

During the election year of 1864, it was frequently suggested to Lincoln that he step aside, not run for reelection, and let another candidate have the White House. Often, he responded with the following:

"I have not permitted myself, gentlemen, to conclude that I am the best man in the country, but I am reminded, in this connection, of a story of an old Dutch farmer who remarked to a companion once that 'it was not best to swap horses when crossing streams.'"

After hearing a comment that the two leading political parties frequently seemed to reverse

6

their platforms so much that they began sounding like their rival, Lincoln responded:

"I remember once being much amused at seeing two partially intoxicated men engage in a fight with their greatcoats on, which, after a long and rather harmless contest, ended in each having fought himself *out* of his own coat, and *into* that of the other's."

DECISIVENESS
Just prior to the onset of the Civil War, when asked about the constant demands that the South was making of the North, Lincoln justified his firm stance by telling the following brief story:

"That reminds me of a dispute that once occurred between my two sons. One of them had a toy that the other wanted and demanded in terms emphatic and boisterous. At length he was told to let his brother have it in order to quiet him. 'No, sir,' was the sturdy response, 'I must have it to quiet myself.'"

A gentleman from Virginia advised the president to surrender Forts Sumter and Pickens and all government property in the Southern states. Lincoln, however, wouldn't hear of it:

"Do you remember the fable of the lion and the woodman's daughter? Well, Aesop wrote that a lion was very much in love with a woodman's daughter. The fair maid referred him to her father. The lion applied for the girl. The father replied: "Your teeth are too long." The lion went to a dentist and had them extracted. Returning, he asked for his bride. "No," said the woodman, "your claws are too long." Going back to the dentist, he had them drawn. Then he returned to claim his bride, and the woodman, seeing that he was unarmed, beat out his brains.

"May it not be so with me, if I give up all that is asked?"

A group of concerned politicians from out West gained an audience with Lincoln and began criticizing the president's handling of various issues. When they started chiding his direction of the administration, Lincoln cut them off by telling this story:

"Gentlemen, suppose all the property you were worth was in gold, and this you had placed in the hands of [a man] to carry across the Niagara River on a rope. Would you shake the cable and keep shouting at him: 'Stand up a little straighter, stoop a little more, go a little faster, go a little slower, lean a little more to the south'? No, you would hold your breath as well as your tongue and keep your hands off until he got safely over.

"The government is carrying an enormous weight. Untold treasure is in our hands. Don't badger us. Keep silent and we will get you safely across."

During a cabinet meeting, Lincoln found himself in the minority about the issue of whether or not to let other nations become involved in the Union's struggle to preserve the nation. "I don't propose to argue this matter," said the president, "because arguments have no effect upon men whose opinions are fixed and whose minds are made up. But this little story of mine will make some things which now are in the dark show up more clearly."

"Gentlemen, the situation just now reminds me of a fix I got into some thirty years or so ago when I was peddling 'notions' on the way from Indiana to Illinois. I didn't have a large stock, but I charged large prices, and I made money. Just before we left Indiana and crossed into Illinois, we came across a small farmhouse full of nothing but children. These ranged in years from seventeen years to seventeen months, and all were in tears. The mother of the family was red-headed and red-faced, and the whip she held in her right hand led to the inference that she had been chastising her brood. The father of the family, a meek-looking, mild-mannered, tow-headed chap, was standing in the front doorway, awaiting—to all appearances—his turn to feel the thong.

"I thought there wasn't much use in asking the head of that house if she wanted any 'notions.' She was too busy. It was evident an insurrection had been in progress, but it was pretty well quelled when I got there. The mother had about suppressed it with an iron hand, but she was not running any risks. She kept a keen and wary eye upon all the children, not forgetting an occasional glance at the 'old man' in the doorway.

"She saw me as I came up, and from her look I thought she was of the opinion that I intended to interfere. Advancing to the doorway, and roughly pushing her husband aside, she demanded my business.

"'Nothing, madam,' I answered as gently as possible. 'I merely dropped in as I came along to see how things were going.'

"'Well, you needn't wait,' was the reply in an irritated way. 'There's trouble here, an' lots of it, too, but I kin manage my own affairs without the help of outsiders. This is jest a family row, but I'll teach these brats their places if I have to lick the hide off every one of them. I don't do much talkin', but I run this house, an' I don't want no one sneakin' 'round tryin' to find out how I do it, either.'

"That's the case here with us. We must let the other nations know that we propose to settle our family row in our own way and 'teach these brats [the seceding states] their places if we have to lick the hide off each and every one of them.' And, like the old woman, we don't want any sneakin' 'round by other countries who would like to find out how we are able to do it, either."

An adviser mentioned to Lincoln that certain political factions were opposed to any negotiations with the South because they *had started the trouble, were entirely responsible for the consequences, and deserved what was coming to them. Lincoln's response was more congenial:*

11

"This reminds me of a story told out in Illinois where I lived. There was a vicious bull in a pasture and a neighbor passing through the field. The animal took after him. He ran to a tree and got there in time to save himself, and being able to run around the tree faster than the bull, he managed to seize him by the tail. The bull, seeing himself at a disadvantage, pawed the earth and scattered gravel for awhile, then broke into a full run, bellowing at every jump. The man held on to his tail, cussing him and asking the question—'Damn you, who commenced this fuss?' Now, our plain duty is to settle the fuss we have before us, without reference to who commenced it."

FLEXIBILITY

Secretary of War Edwin M. Stanton cornered the president and explained to him that he had received a wire asking for urgent instructions and, though he didn't totally understand the request, gave the go-ahead. "I suppose you meant that it was all right if it was good for him and all wrong if it was not," replied Lincoln.

"That reminds me of a story about a horse that was sold at the crossroads near where I once lived. The horse was supposed to be fast, and quite a number of people were present at the time appointed for the sale. A small boy was employed to ride the horse backward and forward to exhibit his points. One of the would-be buyers followed the boy down the road and asked him confidentially if the horse had a splint. 'Well, mister,' said the boy, 'if it's good for him he has got it, but if it isn't good for him, he hasn't.'"

In a political debate, Lincoln's opponent had cleverly evaded answering a question on an important issue, to which Lincoln remarked:

"He reminds me of a hunter I once knew who recognized the fact that in summer the deer were red and in winter gray, and at one season, therefore, a deer might resemble a calf. The hunter had brought down one at long range when it was hard to see the difference, and boasting of his own marksmanship had said: 'I shot at it so as to hit it if it was a deer and miss it if a calf.'"

GET TO THE CORE; DON'T WASTE TIME
When he was presented with a proposal to disrupt the cotton industry—the South's main cash crop—Lincoln immediately accepted the idea and ordered that the plan be implemented:

"The Confederacy is like Bill Sikes' dog," said Lincoln. "Old Bill Sikes had a yellow dog, a worthless cur. His strong point was to run out and bark at passersby and scare horses and children. The boys in the neighborhood decided to have some fun with the no-account canine brute. They procured a small stick of giant powder, inserted a cap and fuse into it, wrapped a piece of meat around it, lit the fuse, laid out the little joker on the sidewalk, whistled, and climbed the fence to see the fun. Out comes the dog with his usual 'bow, wow.' He scented the meat and swallowed the bundle. In a few seconds there was a terrible explosion. Dog meat was flying in all directions.

"Out came Sikes from the house, bareheaded. 'What in hell's up?' yelled Old Bill. 'Why, the dog's up,' cried the boys on the fence. While Old Bill was gazing around in wonderment, something dropped at his feet. He picked it up and found that it was his dog's tail. While looking sorrowfully at the appendage of his departed friend, he exclaimed: 'Well, I'll be damned if I think Tige'll amount to much after this as a dog.'

"And so it would be with the Confederacy. Take all the cotton away from them, and it wouldn't amount to shucks."

When he was told of an ill-conceived plan for a military expedition down the Yazoo River, Lincoln reacted negatively, termed it a waste of time, and told the following story to illustrate his point:

"There was a man in Illinois a good many years since that was troubled with an old sow and her pigs—again and again the old man and his sons drove her out and repeatedly found her in the lot. One day he and his boys searched about and found that she got into the lot through a certain hollow log that had been placed in the fence; they took out this log and built up the fence by placing the log a little differently than before, and the next day, what was the astonishment of the old lady to find that she and her litter came out of the log outside of the field instead of inside.

"It is just so with the Yazoo River expedition. It comes out of the same side of the log."

A Virginia farmer once called on President Lincoln and asked to be reimbursed for damage done to his farm by Union soldiers. "Why, my dear sir," replied Lincoln, "I couldn't think of such a thing. If I considered individual cases, I wouldn't have time to get anything done." But, the farmer continued to pester the president until Lincoln finally told this story:

"You remind me of Old Jock Chase, out in Illinois. You see, Jock—I knew him like a brother—used to be a lumberman on the Illinois, and he was steady and sober and the best raftsman on the river. It was quite a trick twenty-five years ago to take the logs over the rapids; but he was skillful with a raft and always kept her straight in the channel. Finally, a steamboat was put on, and Jock—he's dead now, poor fellow!—was made captain of her. One day, when the boat was plunging and wallowing along the boiling current, and Jock's utmost vigilance was being exercised to keep her in the narrow channel, a boy pulled at his coattail and hailed him with, 'Say, mister captain! I wish you would jest stop your boat a minute—I've lost my apple overboard!'"

Lincoln once squelched a particularly offensive heckler by suddenly stopping his speech, turning directly toward the offender, and noting to the audience:

"This noisy friend reminds me of a certain steamboat that used to run on the Illinois

River. It was an energetic boat, was always busy. When they built it, however, they made one serious mistake, this error being in the relative sizes of the boiler and the whistle. The latter was usually busy, too, and people were aware that it was in existence.

"This particular boiler to which I have reference was a six-foot one and did all that was required of it in the way of pushing the boat along; but as the builders of the vessel had made the whistle a six-foot one, the consequence was that every time the whistle blew the boat had to stop."

During his reelection bid in 1864, perhaps commenting about all the negative attacks on his character without reference to the issues, Lincoln told the following story:

"A traveler on the frontier found himself out of his reckoning one night in a most inhospitable region. A terrific thunderstorm came up to add to his trouble. He floundered along until his horse at length gave out. The lightning afforded him the only clue to his way, but the peals of thunder were frightful. One bolt, which seemed to crash the earth beneath him, brought him to his knees. By no means a praying man, his petition was short and to the point—'O Lord, if it is all the same to you, give us a little more light and a little less noise!'"

As a lawyer, Lincoln once noted in court that excessively long documents are a waste of time and frequently the work of lethargic lawyers.

"It's like the lazy preacher who used to read very long sermons. When asked how so lazy a man used to write such long sermons, one of his deacons said, 'Oh, he gets to writing and is too lazy to stop.'"

When a gentleman gained access to Lincoln in the White House, he began reading aloud several letters of recommendation. But before he was half through with the documents, the president cried out:

"Oh, stop! You are like the man who killed the dog. This man had a vicious animal which he determined to dispatch, and accordingly knocked out his brains with a club. He continued striking the dog until a friend stayed his hand, exclaiming, 'You needn't strike him any-more, the dog is dead; you killed him at the first blow.' 'Oh, yes,' said he, 'I know that; but I believe in punishment after death.'"

During a cabinet meeting the subject of art was discussed, and a reference was made to Thomas D. Jones, the sculptor, who had made a bust of the president a few years earlier. Lincoln grinned from ear to ear and piped up with the following story:

"Thomas D. Jones, the sculptor, tells a good story of General Winfield Scott, of whom he once made a bust. Having a fine subject to start with, he succeeded in giving great satisfaction. At the closing sitting he attempted to define and elaborate the lines and markings of the face. The general sat patiently; but when he came to see the result, his countenance indicat-ed decided displeasure. 'Why, Jones, what have you been doing?' he asked. 'Oh,' rejoined the sculptor, 'not much, I confess, General; I have been working out the details of the face a little more this morning.' 'Details!' exclaimed the general, warmly; 'Damn the details! Why, my man, you are spoiling the bust!'"

HONESTY AND INTEGRITY

In 1863, when the assistant attorney general told the president that U.S. marshals preferred to tap a legal defense fund rather than seek aid from district attorneys, Lincoln quickly responded with this story:

"Yes, they will now all be after the money and be content with nothing else. They are like the man in Illinois whose cabin was burned down, and according to the kindly custom of early days in the West, his neighbors all contributed something to start him again. In his case they had been so liberal that he soon found himself better off than before the fire, and he got proud. One day a neighbor brought him a bag of oats, but the fellow refused it with scorn. 'No,' said he, 'I'm not taking oats now. I take nothing but money.'"

HUMAN NATURE

When Great Britain and the United States were squabbling over the Union's capture of the British vessel Trent *with two Confederate commissioners on board, Lincoln's cabinet was greatly concerned about a war erupting between the two nations. A few members even advocated starting a war in an effort to unite the North and South against a common enemy. Lincoln, however, calmly rejected the idea: "One war at a time, gentlemen," he said. And then Lincoln revealed a much more intuitive understanding of the situation with this appropriate story:*

"I remember when I was a lad, there were two fields behind our house separated by a fence. In each field there was a big bulldog, and these dogs spent the whole day racing up and down, snarling and yelping at each other through that fence. One day they both came at the same moment to a hole in it big enough to let either of them through. Well, gentlemen, what do you think they did? They just turned tail and scampered away as fast as they could in opposite directions. Now, England and America are like those bulldogs."

INNOVATION
When the president was asked by a delegation of ministers what he intended to do about slavery, Lincoln responded with the following:

"Gentlemen, I will tell you how it is. The treatment proposed by the officials here for the slavery question is about like what would be proposed by a set of doctors for a man with a large, ugly wart on his person. He consults a number of physicians about it, and they all agree that it must come off. About the method of removing it, they do not agree. One says the best way is to put the knife into it, and with the knife remove it. One advises powerful external applications with a view to its removal. Another thinks the better way is to put a cord tightly around it and every day draw it tighter, until at last a severance will of itself occur. That, gentlemen, is just the way it is here with us. We are all agreed that slavery is a wart on the government. We are all agreed that it must come off. We are not agreed about how to do it."

"Every man has his own peculiar and particular way of getting at and doing things," Lincoln said one day, *"and he is often criticized because that way is not the one adopted by others.*

"That reminds me of a fellow out in Illinois who had better luck in getting prairie chickens than anyone in the neighborhood. He had a rusty old gun no other man dared to handle. He never seemed to exert himself, being listless and indifferent when out after game, but he always brought home all the chickens he could carry, while some of the others, with their finely trained dogs and latest improved fowling pieces, came home alone.

"'How is it, Jake?' inquired one sportsman, who, although a good shot and knew something about hunting, was often unfortunate, "that you never come home without a lot of birds?'

"Jake grinned, half closed his eyes, and replied: 'Oh, I don't know that there's anything queer about it. I jes' go ahead an' git 'em.'

"'Yes, I know you do, but how do you do it?'

"'You'll tell.'

"'Honest, Jake, I won't say a word. Hope to drop dead this minute.'

"'Never say nothing if I tell you?'

"'Cross my heart three times.'

"This reassured Jake, who put his mouth close to the ear of his eager questioner and said in a whisper: 'All you got to do is jes' to hide in a fence corner an' make a noise like a turnip. That'll bring the chickens every time.'"

"A colonel once proposed to his men that he should do all the swearing of the regiment. They assented; and for months no instance was known of the violation of the promise. The colonel had a teamster named John Todd, who, as the roads were not always the best, had some difficulty in commanding his temper and his tongue. John happened to be driving a muleteam through a series of mud pools a little

23

worse than usual when, unable to restrain himself any longer, he burst forth in a volley of energetic oaths. The colonel took notice of the offense and brought John to an account. 'John,' said he, 'didn't you promise to let me do all the swearing of the regiment?' 'Yes, I did, Colonel,' he replied, 'but the fact was the swearing had to be done then or not at all, and you weren't there to do it.'"

MOTIVATION

When Lincoln was asked what he was going to do about Secretary of the Treasury Salmon P. Chase's driving ambition to become president, he grinned and told the following story:

"My brother and I were once plowing corn, I driving the horse, and he holding the plow. The horse was lazy, but on one occasion he rushed across the field so that I, with my long legs, could scarcely keep pace with him. On reaching the end of the furrow, I found an enormous chinfly fastened upon him, and knocked him off. My brother asked me what I did that for. I told him I didn't want the old horse bitten in that way. 'Why,' said my brother, 'that's all that made him go.' Now, if Mr. Chase has a presidential chin-fly biting him, I'm not going to knock him off if it will only make his department go."

PATIENCE—AVOID RASHNESS

When the president was asked why he wasn't doing anything to counter Chase's efforts to become the Republican presidential nominee in 1864, Lincoln responded:

"I'm not afraid of Chase; he's too anxious and too willing, and that sort of thing doesn't go well in courting and in some other things. Chase reminds me of a fellow student of mine. He was a fine fellow but rather fast and inclined to keep questionable company. We were finally much pleased to hear that he had formed the acquaintance of one of the nicest girls in the town and that everything seemed to be tending toward a very satisfactory ending. There came a day, however, when he became despondent. We sought to learn the trouble. 'I've lost her,' was the answer. 'I was in too much of a hurry. I embraced her before I popped the question.' Now that is the trouble with our friend Chase."

When Lincoln was asked by a New Yorker when he was going to emancipate the slaves, the president politely responded with this story:

"Well, you see, we've got to be very cautious how we manage the Negro question. If we're

25

not we shall be like the barber out in Illinois who was shaving a fellow with a hatchet face and lantern jaws like mine. The barber stuck his finger into his customer's mouth to make his cheek stick out, but while shaving away he cut through the fellow's cheek and cut off his own finger. If we are not very careful we shall do as the barber did."

The president was once asked to release a number of men, women, and children who had been arrested by an order from General David Hunter.

"General Hunter reminds me of an old judge who had a propensity for fining offenders, no matter what the offense. On one occasion the regular term of court was not long enough to close all the cases and enable the judge to order fines, so he held an adjourned term for that purpose, and while intently occupied in that agreeable duty the stovepipe fell. Whereupon the judge, enraged at the interruption, without stopping to learn the cause, called out, 'Sheriff, arrest everyone in the room! Mr. Clerk, enter a fine against every one of them!' Then, looking through his spectacles and seeing the crowd, his honor said, 'Stop, Mr. Clerk; enter a fine against everyone in the room, women and children alone excepted.'

"I don't know but this general of mine has a great propensity for arresting as the old judge had for fining people."

One evening when Lincoln was out in the field visiting the troops, a single shot was heard— quickly followed by a thunderous volley of more guns being fired. It was reported back to the president that they were not under attack but that a careless recruit had accidentally discharged his weapon which, in turn, so alarmed the other soldiers that they fired theirs, fearing an assault. Lincoln grinned and said:

"This affair reminds me of an occurrence which once took place in Springfield, Illinois. It happened one third of July night, after quite a number of people from the surrounding county had assembled in town in anticipation of participating in the celebration of the anniversary of our national independence, and after nearly everybody had gone to sleep, with the exception of a few frolicsome young fellows who had been prowling about town until after midnight. They had pretty well exhausted their ingenuity in devising new pranks for fun and mischief, when one of them proposed to bet drinks for the party that he would within five minutes' time make every cock in the whole town crow. The wager was promptly accepted, and the young fellow leaped upon a fence and, slapping his thighs with his open hands, gave forth a vociferous 'cock-a-doodle-do,' which in the stillness of the calm night reverberated like a solitary reply issued from a chicken-roost in a remote suburb, which was soon taken up by others in different directions, and within the brief period specified in the wager probably every cock in the town had repeated the call. But the strangest part of the whole affair was that the sell was not confined to the chickens, for as soon as the crowing commenced, all the boys in the place, who very likely slept with one eye open upon that special occasion, and verily believing the joyful fourth of July had dawned, leaped out of bed, jumped into their clothes, and rushed to the streets, and within less time than it has taken to relate it, firecrackers, pistols, and guns were being discharged from every direction. "

PERSISTENCE

"I am sometimes reminded of Old Mother Partington on the sea beach. A big storm came up, and the waves began to rise till the water came in under her cabin door. She got a broom and went to sweeping it out. But the water rose higher and higher, to her knees, to her waist, at last to her chin. But she kept on sweeping and exclaiming, 'I'll keep on sweeping as long as the broom lasts, and we will see whether the storm or the broom will last the longest.'"

When one of Lincoln's generals complained that his efforts had stalled and asked the president for advice, Lincoln told him to use his own best judgment but to keep moving:

"You see, General, we are like an old acquaintance of mine who settled on a piece of 'galled' prairie. It was a terrible rough place to clear up, but after a while he got a few things growing—here and there a patch of corn, a few hills of beans, and so on. One day a stranger stopped to look at his place and wanted to know how he managed to cultivate so rough a spot. 'Well,' was the reply, 'some of it is pretty rough. The smaller stumps I can generally root out or burn out; but now and then there is an old settler that bothers me, and there is no other way but to plow around it.'

"Now, General, at such a time as this, troublesome cases are constantly coming up, and the only way to get along at all is to plow around them."

Prior to one of the Lincoln-Douglas debates in 1858, an acquaintance expressed concern that Douglas appeared much more flamboyant and confident than he, to which Lincoln smiled and said:

"Sit down. I have a moment to spare and will tell you a story. You have seen two men about to fight? Well, one of them brags about what he means to do. He jumps high in the air, cracking his heels together, smites his fists, and wastes his breath trying to scare somebody. You see the other fellow. He says not a word. His arms are at his sides, his fists are closely doubled up, his head is drawn to the shoulder, and his teeth are set firm together. He is saving his wind for the fight, and as sure as it comes off he will win it or die a-trying."

When he was asked to handle a matter personally rather than delegating it to one of his cabinet members, Lincoln defended his cabinet members by comparing them to fighting dogs:

"A man in his neighborhood had a small bull-terrier that could whip all the dogs of the neighborhood. The owner of a large dog which the terrier had whipped asked the owner of the terrier how it happened that the terrier whipped every dog he encountered. 'That,' said the owner of the terrier, 'is no mystery to me. Your dog and other dogs get half through a fight before they are ready. Now, my dog is always mad!'"

VISION

When one of Lincoln's generals presented a plan that entailed sending an army into the deep South, the president thoughtfully expressed his concern with a story:

"That reminds me of a cooper out my way, new at the trade and much annoyed by the head of the barrel falling in as he was hooping in the staves around it. But the bright idea occurred to him to put his boy in to hold up the cover. Only when the job was completed by this inner support, the new problem arose: how to get the boy out?"

Then Lincoln turned to the general and said: "Your plan is feasible, sir; but how are you to get the boy out?"

———

As President Lincoln and General Grant were inspecting the Dutch Gap Canal at City Point,

Lincoln suddenly turned to the general and exclaimed:

"Grant, do you know what this reminds me of? Out in Springfield, there was a blacksmith who one day, not having much to do, took a piece of soft iron and attempted to weld it into an agricultural implement but discovered that the iron would not hold out. Then, he decided it would make a claw hammer, but having too much iron attempted to make an ax, but decided after working a while that there was not enough iron left. Finally, becoming disgusted, he filled the forge full of coal and brought the iron to a white heat; then with his tongs he lifted it from the bed of coals, and thrusting it into a tub of water nearby, exclaimed with an oath: 'Well, if I can't make anything else of you, I will make a fizzle anyhow.'

"I was afraid that was about what we had done with the Dutch Gap Canal."

"A man on foot, with his clothes in a bundle, coming to a running stream which he must ford, made elaborate preparations by stripping off his garments, adding them to his bundle, and tying all to the top of a stick, which enabled him to raise the bundle high above his head to keep them dry during the crossing. He then fearlessly waded in and carefully made his way across the rippling stream and found it in no place up to his ankles."

President Lincoln once stated that the Trent affair had given him several sleepless nights and that releasing the two captured commissioners was "a pretty bitter pill to swallow. But I contented myself with believing that England's triumph in the matter would be short-lived, and that after ending our war successfully we should be so powerful that we could call England to account for all the embarrassments she had inflicted upon us. I felt a good deal like the sick man in Illinois who was told he probably hadn't many days longer to live, and he ought to make peace with any enemies he might have. He said the man he hated worst of all was a fellow named Brown, in the next village, and he guessed he had better commence on him first. So Brown was sent for, and when he came the sick man began to say, in a voice as meek as Moses', that he wanted to die at peace with all his fellow creatures and hoped he and Brown could now shake hands and bury all their animosity. The scene was becoming altogether too pathetic for Brown, who had to get out his handkerchief and wipe the gathering tears from his eyes. It wasn't long before he melted and gave his hand to his neighbor [in friendship]. After a parting that would have softened the heart of a grindstone, Brown had about reached the room door when the sick man rose up on his elbow and said, 'But see here, Brown, if I should happen to get well—that old grudge stands!'

"So I thought if this nation should happen to get well, we might want that old grudge against England to stand."

"Mr. Speaker, this gentleman reminds me of an old friend of mine—a grizzled frontiersman with shaggy overhanging brows and spectacles. One morning, on looking out of his cabin door, the old gentleman thought he saw a squirrel frisking on a tree near the house. He took down his gun and fired at it, but the squirrel paid no attention. Again and again he fired, getting more mystified and more mortified at each failure. After a round dozen shots he threw down the gun, muttering that there was something wrong with the rifle.

"'Rifle's all right,' declared his son who had been watching him. 'Rifle's all right, but where's your squirrel?'

"'Don't you see him?' thundered the old man, pointing out the exact spot.

"'No, I don't,' was the candid answer. Then, turning and staring into his father's face, the boy broke into a jubilant shout. 'Now I see your squirrel! You've been firing at a bug on your eyebrow.'"

<hr>

President Lincoln told the following story to General Grant after calling him aside to discuss his appointment as general-in-chief:

"At one time there was a great war among the animals," Lincoln began, "and one side had great difficulty in getting a commander who had sufficient confidence in himself. Finally, they found a monkey by the name of Jocko who said that he thought he could command their army if his tail could be made a little longer. So they got more tail and spliced it onto his caudal appendage. He looked at it admiringly and then thought he ought to have a little more still. This was added, and again he called for more. The splicing process was repeated many times until they had coiled Jocko's tail around the room, filling all the space. Still he called for more tail and, there being no other place to coil it, they began wrapping it around his shoulders. He continued his call for more, and they kept on winding the additional tail about him until its weight broke him down."

General Grant then assured Lincoln that he knew what the president was talking about and that he would not call for more troops unless absolutely necessary.

In 1858, Lincoln once related to a friend that he thought Stephen A. Douglas was being short-sighted in his dogmatic quest for reelection to the Senate—and was not looking ahead to the presidency in 1860.

"There was a fine old farmer out our way who had a fair daughter and a fine apple tree, each of which he prized as 'the apple of his eye.'

"One of the courters 'sparking' up for her hand was a dashing young fellow, while his rival next in consequence was but a plain person in face and speech whom, however, the farmer favored, no doubt from 'Like liking Like.' (The dashing young chap was afterward hanged, by the way.) One day, the two happened to meet at the farmer's fence. It enclosed his orchard where the famous Baldwin flourished. That year was the off-year, but, as sometimes occurs, the yield, though sparse, comprised some rare beauties. There was one, a 'whopper,' on which the farmer had centered his care as if for a human pet. He looked after it well and saw it heave up into plumpness with joy. When Dashing Jack came up, he saw his fellow beau just hefting a stone.

"'What are you going to do with that rock?' asked he, careless-like, though somehow or other interested, too, as we are in anything a rival does in the neighborhood of our sweetheart.

"'Why, I was just a-going to see if I could knock off that big red apple, that is all.'

"'You can't do it in the first try!' taunted the dasher.

"'Neither can you. Bet!'

"Jack would not make any bet with plain John, but he took up a pebble and, contemptuously whistling through his fine regular teeth, sure as fate knocked the big Baldwin in the girth and sent it hopping off the limb. Then, as the victors are entitled to the spoil, he went in, picked up the fruit and was walking up to the house when whom should he run up against but the old man! Now, to see *that* apple off and to see any man munching it like a crab was too much for his nerves. He did not stop to say [anything] but, wearing these here copper-toed boots such as were a novelty in that section 'bout then, he raised the young man so [far] that he and the apple, to which he clung, landed on the other side of the fence.

"Then? Well, then, the plain John swallowed a snicker or two and went right in, condoled with the old fellow on his loss of the pet Baldy, and asked for the girl right slick.

"Dashing Jack got the apple, but it was the other who got the gal."

PART
II

Lincoln Stories
for
Practical Leadership
Situations

For the Leader Who Is Constantly Rushed by His Subordinates from One Meeting to Another.

Well, I feel about as the convict did in Illinois when he was going to the gallows. Passing along the road in custody of the sheriff and seeing the people who were eager for the execution crowding and jostling one another past him, he at last called out, "Boys, you needn't be in such a hurry to get ahead. There won't be any fun till I get there."

For People Who Try to Postpone a Meeting Because They're Not Prepared.

It's very natural they should want to postpone. There were two men in jail here a few weeks since, under sentence of death, and their friends were anxious to have the hanging postponed.

To Illustrate How You Feel When Those "Glossy" Budget Presentations Are Over and You Can Finally Get Back to Basics.

I used to know a little girl out West who sometimes was inclined to eat too much. One day she ate a good many more raisins than she should have and followed them up with a quantity of other goodies such as cake, candy, ice cream, and the like. They made her very sick, and she threw up all the goodies. After a time the raisins began to come.

She gasped and looked at her mother and said: "Well, I will be better now I guess, for I have got down to the raisins."

To Quell Rumors.

Some years ago two Irishmen landed in this country and, taking the way out into the interior after labor, came suddenly near a pond of water, and to their great horror they heard some bullfrogs singing their usual song—R-i-b-e-t!—R-i-b-e-t!—R-i-b-e-t! They listened and trembled, and feeling the necessity of bravery they clutched their shillelagh and crept cautiously forward, straining their eyes in every direction to catch a glimpse of the enemy, but he was not to be found. At last a happy idea came to the most forward one, and he sprang to his mate and exclaimed, "Jamie, it is my opinion it's nothing but a *noise.*"

Breaking Up People Who Are "Shooting the Breeze" When They Should Be Working.

You people remind me of the boy who set a hen on forty-three eggs. You see, a youngster put forty-three eggs under a hen and then rushed in and told his mother what he had done.

"But a hen can't set on forty-three eggs," replied the mother.

"No, I guess she can't, but I just wanted to see her spread herself."

That's what I wanted to see you people do when I came in.

For Those Times When the Boss Happens to Walk by Your Office Just When You Pick Up a Magazine or Relax for a Few Minutes.

That is very like the story I heard of a man driving about the country in an open buggy, caught at night by a pouring rain. Passing a farmhouse, a man, apparently struggling with the effects of whisky, thrust his head out of a window and shouted loudly: "Hello!"

The traveler stopped, for all of his hurry for shelter, and asked what was wanted. "Nothing of you!" was the blunt reply.

"Well, why are you shouting 'Hello' when people are passing?" angrily asked the traveler.

"Well, why are you passing by when people are shouting 'Hello'?"

Getting Rid of Advice-Givers and Office-Seekers.

This makes me think of the Irishman whose horse kicked up and caught his foot in the stirrup. "Arrah!" he said. "If you are going to get on, I will get off."

Gentlemen, the conditions in that department put me in mind of the time that a young friend and myself tried to court the two daughters of a peppery widow living near our homes. The old lady kept a lot of hounds.

We had not been in the house long before one of the hounds came into the room and lay down by the fire. In a little while another one came to the door. He didn't get in, for the old lady gave him a kick, saying: "Get out of here! There's too many dogs in here now!"

We concluded to court some other girls.

46

Judge, this reminds me of an anecdote which I heard a son of yours tell in Burlington, Iowa. He was trying to enforce upon his hearers the truth of the old adage that three moves is worse than a fire. As an illustration he gave an account of a family who started from Western Pennsylvania, pretty well off in this world's goods when they started. But they moved and moved, having less and less every time they moved, till after a while they could carry everything in one wagon. He said that the chickens of the family got so used to being moved, that whenever they saw the wagon sheets brought out, they laid themselves on their backs and crossed their legs, ready to be tied. Now, gentlemen, if I were to listen to every committee that comes in at that door, I had just as well cross my hands and let you tie me.

Gentlemen, you are like the soldiers of the Crusades who discarded their homes and comfort, suffered the tortures of long marches, were assailed by sickness, and were at all times ready to give their lives for their beliefs. The army of the Crusades once attacked a walled city. Under fierce fires of arrows and huge catapults, they dragged their scaling ladders and placed them against the ramparts. With rapidly thinning ranks, they mounted round-by-round, and ultimately some of them reached the top. The tide of the contest turned in their favor, and the besieged city was taken. But, gentlemen, those heroic soldiers who were first on top of the walls didn't get the offices.

My friend, let me tell you something: you are a farmer, I believe; if not, you will understand me. Suppose you had a large cattle yard full of all sorts of cattle, cows, oxen, and bulls, and you kept selling your cows and oxen, taking good care of your bulls. By and by, you would find that you had nothing but a yard full of old bulls, good for nothing under heaven, and it will be just so with my army if I don't stop making brigadier generals.

Gentlemen, I must tell you a little story I read one day when I was minding a mudscow in one of the bayous near Yazoo. A certain king had a minister upon whose judgment he always depended, just as I do upon my friend here [pointing to Secretary Seward].

Now, it happened that one day the king took it into his head to go a hunting, and after summoning his nobles and making the necessary preparations, he summoned the minister and asked him if it would rain. The minister told him it would not, and he and his nobles departed.

While journeying along they met a countryman on a jackass. He advised them to return. "Because," he said, "it will certainly rain." They smiled contemptuously upon him and passed on. Before they had gone many miles, however, they had reason to regret not having taken the rustic's advice, as a heavy shower came up and they were drenched to the skin.

When they had returned to the palace, the king reprimanded the minister severely.

"I met a countryman," said he, "and he knows a great deal more than you, for he told me it would rain, whereas you told me it would not."

The king then gave him his walking papers and sent for the countryman.

"Tell me," said the king, "how you knew it would rain."

"I didn't know," said the rustic. "My jackass told me."

"And how, pray, did he tell you?" asked the king.

"By pricking up his ears, your majesty," returned the rustic.

The king sent the countryman away, and procuring the jackass of him, put him (the jackass) in the place the minister had filled.

And here is where the king made a great mistake. How so, you ask? Because ever since that time, every jackass wants an office.

When There Are Too Many Subordinates Who Want to Be Promoted.

That reminds me of a story I heard in a small town in Illinois where I once lived. Every man in the town owned a fast horse, each one considering his own the fastest, so to decide the matter there was to be a trial of all the horses to take place at the same time. One old man living in the town known as "Uncle" was selected as umpire. When it was over and each one anxious for his decision, the old man putting his hands behind his back said: "I have come to one conclusion, that where there are so many fast horses in our little town, none of them are any great shakes."

For the Employee Who Has to Let His Boss Know How Hard His Job Is and Always "Screams" to Get Attention.

This person is like the boy I once saw at a launching. When everything was ready, they picked out a boy and sent him under the ship to knock away the trigger and let her go.

At the critical moment, everything depended on the boy. He had to do the job well by a direct, vigorous blow and then lie flat and keep still while the boat slid over him.

The boy did everything right, but he yelled as if he were being murdered from the time he got under the keel until he got out. I thought the hide was all scraped off his back, but he wasn't hurt at all.

The master of the yard told me that this boy was always chosen for that job, that he did his work well, that he never had been hurt, but that he always squealed in that way. That's just the way with the governor. Make up your minds that he is not hurt, that he is doing his work right, and pay no attention to his squealing.

You see, he only wants to make you understand how hard his task is and that he is on hand performing it.

For People Who Just Don't Seem to Get the Message.

Grown up men and women, even nations, at times are like the little girl who asked her mother if she could run out and play. The mother refused, and the girl begged harder, kept teasing till the mother gave her a whipping. When that was over the girl said, "Now, Ma, I can surely run out and play."

Turning Down a Transfer to an Undesirable Location.

One terribly stormy night in bleak December, a United States vessel was wrecked off the coast of Jersey, and every soul save one went down with the doomed craft. This one survivor seized a floating mast and was washed toward the shore, while innumerable kindhearted laborers of the Camden and Amboy railroad clustered on the beach with ropes and boats. Slowly the unhappy mariner drifted to land, and as he exhaustedly caught at the rope thrown to him, the kindly natives uttered an encouraging cheer.

"You are saved!" they shouted. "You are saved and must show the conductor your ticket!"

With the sea still boiling about him, the drowning stranger resisted the efforts to haul him ashore.

"Stop!" said he, in faint tones. "Tell me where I am! What country is this?"

They answered, "New Jersey."

Scarcely had the name been uttered when the wretched stranger let go of the rope, exclaiming as he did so, "I guess I'll float a little farther."

To Illustrate a Dishonest Manager Who Tries to Make Others Believe He Is a "People Person" by Saying: "I've Never Yet Had a Man Under Me Quit." In Reality, However, He Either Fires People or They Request Transfers.

Well, that reminds me of a hotel keeper down at St. Louis who boasted that he never had a death in his hotel, for whenever a guest was dying in his house he carried him out to die in the gutter.

For People Who Smile and Then Stab You in the Back.

Did you ever see a tree that was being killed by a vine which covered its trunk? It's very beautiful, but it's like the smiles of certain men. It decorates the ruin it makes.

To Illustrate People Who Will Support Whatever Position That Benefits Them the Most.

James Quarles, a distinguished lawyer of Tennessee, was trying a case, and, after producing his evidence, rested. Whereupon the defense produced a witness who swore Quarles completely out of court, and a verdict was rendered accordingly. After the trial, one of his friends came to him and said:

"Why didn't you get that feller to swar on your side?"

"I didn't know anything about him," replied Quarles.

"I might have told you about him," said the friend, "for he would swar for you jest as hard as he'd swar for the other side. That's his business. Judge, that feller takes in swaring for a livin'!"

To Illustrate People Who Do Wrong and Then Accuse Others.

That reminds me of the young man who had an aged mother and father owning considerable property. The young man, being an only son and believing that the old people had outlived their usefulness, assassinated them both. He was accused, tried, and convicted of the murder. When the judge came to pass sentence upon him and called upon him to give any reason he might have why the sentence of death should not be passed upon him, he with great promptness replied that he hoped the court would be lenient to him because he was a poor orphan!

A ruffian made an unprovoked assault in the street upon a quiet citizen, at the same time drawing his revolver, but the assaulted party made a sudden spring and wrested the weapon from the hands of the would-be assassin. "Stop!" said the latter. "Give me back that pistol; you have no right to my property."

To Illustrate Greedy People.

That reminds me of the farmer who asserted:

"I ain't greedy 'bout land. I only wants what joins mine."

A Good Illustration for When Something Doesn't Seem Right but You Can't Quite Put Your Finger on It.

My opinion on the tariff reminds me of a story. When I was a clerk in a grocery store in New Salem, down in Menard County, a man came in and said to the storekeeper:

"I want a nickel's worth of ginger-snaps." When they were laid out on the counter, the customer changed his mind and said: "I'll have a glass of cider instead." He drank the cider and turned toward the door. "Here, Bill," said the storekeeper, "ain't you goin' to pay for that cider?" The reply came back: "Didn't I give you the gingersnaps for it?" "Well, then, pay me for the gingersnaps." "But I never ate your gingersnaps," was the quick answer. The storekeeper grudgingly admitted that he had told the truth but added he had lost something somehow in the deal.

So it is with the tariff. Somebody loses; but I don't know as yet who it is.

For That One Thing That Tends to Get the Best of You.

I feel very much like the steam doctor, who said he could get along well enough in his way of practice with almost every case, but he was always a little puzzled when it came to mending a broken leg.

A Good Reply When Told About Some Dishonest Practices in Your Organization.

I have a story which I think applicable to this case, and which is expressive of my feelings.

When I was out West, I knew an old farmer who had settled in a dense forest not far from my house. He cleared about an acre of land, built a cabin, and brought his wife and children there and seemed to be living very happily and doing finely. All the trees had been cut down except one old monarch, which he had left to shade his house.

It was a majestic-looking tree and apparently perfect in every part—tall, straight, and of immense size—the grand old sentinel of his forest home.

One morning, while at work in his garden, he saw a squirrel run up the tree into a hole and thought the tree might be hollow. He proceeded to examine it carefully and, much to his surprise, he found that the stately monarch that he had spared for its beauty and grandeur to be the pride and protection of his little farm was hollow from top to bottom. Only a rim of sound wood remained, barely sufficient to support its weight; all the inside was rotten. What was he to do? If he cut it down, it would do great damage with its great length and spreading branches. If he let it remain, his family was in constant danger. In a storm it might fall, or the wind might blow it down, and his house and children be crushed by it. What should he do? As he turned away, he said sadly: "I wish I had never seen that squirrel."

And gentlemen, I wish we had never seen what we have today.

On Dealing with Setbacks, Disappointment, or Failure.

I knew a fellow once who had saved up fifteen hundred dollars and had placed it in a banking establishment. The bank soon failed, and he afterward received 10 percent of his investment. He then took his one hundred and fifty dollars and deposited it in a savings bank, where he was sure it would be safe. In a short time this bank also failed, and he received at the final settlement 10 percent on the amount deposited. When the fifteen dollars was paid over to him, he held it in his hand and looked at it thoughtfully; then he said, "Now, darn you, I have got you reduced to a portable shape, so I'll put you in my pocket."

Illustrating Fright as a Motivator.

I never knew but one fellow who could move like that, and he was a young man out in Illinois. He had been sparking a girl, much against the wishes of her father. In fact, the old man took such a dislike to him that he threatened to shoot him if he ever caught him around his premises again.

One evening the young man learned that the girl's father had gone to the city, and he ventured out to the house. He was sitting in the parlor, with his arm around Betsy's waist, when he suddenly spied the old man coming around the corner of the house with a shotgun. Leaping through a window into the garden, he started down a path at the top of his speed. He was a long-legged fellow and could run like greased lightning. Just then a jackrabbit jumped up in the path in front of him. In about two leaps he overtook the rabbit. Giving it a kick that sent it high in the air, he exclaimed: "Git out of the road, gosh dern you, and let somebody run that knows how."

Sink or Swim; Throw People in and See If They Survive.

That reminds me of an old friend in Illinois who had a crop of potatoes and did not want to dig them. So he told a neighbor that he would turn in his hogs and let them dig them for themselves. "But," said the neighbor, "the frost will soon be in the ground, and when the soil is hard frozen, what will they do then?" To which the worthy farmer replied, "Let 'em root!"

Illustrating Overexaggeration or Grandiose Statements.

This reminds me of a notorious liar who attained such a reputation as an exaggerator that he finally instructed his servant to stop him when his tongue was running too rapidly by pulling his coat or touching his feet. One day the master was relating wonders he had seen in Europe and described a building which was about a mile long and a half-mile high. Just then the servant's heel came down on the narrator's toes, and he stopped abruptly. One of the listeners asked how broad this remarkable building might be; the narrator modestly replied, "About a foot!"

Illustrating the Hazards of Overconfidence.

This situation reminds me of three or four fellows out near Athens (Menard County), who went coon hunting one day. After being out some time, the dogs treed a coon, which was soon discovered in the extreme top of a very tall oak tree. They had only one gun, a rifle, and after some discussion as to who was the best shot, one was decided on who took the rifle, and, getting in a good position, the coon being in plain view, lying close on a projecting limb, and at times moving slowly along, the man fired, but the coon was still on the limb. A small bunch of leaves from just in front of the coon fluttered down.

The surprise and indignation of the other fellows was boundless, and all sorts of epithets were heaped on the best shot. "Well," he said, "you see, boys, by gum, I sighted just a leetle ahead and 'lowed for the durn'd thing crawling."

That reminds me of a pleasant little affair that occurred out in Illinois. A gentleman was nominated for supervisor. On leaving home on the morning of election, he said:

"Wife, tonight you shall sleep with the supervisor of this town."

The election passed, and the confident gentleman was defeated. The wife heard the news before her defeated spouse returned home. She immediately dressed for going out and awaited her husband's return when she met him at the door.

"Wife, where are you going at this time of night?" he exclaimed.

"Going?" she replied. "Why, you told me this morning that I should tonight sleep with the supervisor of this town, and I was going to his house."

How to Head Off or "Decline" a Potential Rival.

How would it look if I were to "decline" Chase? Well, I don't know exactly how it might be done, but I had in mind the story of two Democratic candidates for senator down in "Egypt," Illinois, in early political times. That section of the state was almost solidly Democratic, as you know, and nobody but Democrats were candidates for office. The two Democratic candidates for senator met each other in joint debate each day and gradually became more and more exasperated at each other until their discussions were simply disgraceful wrangles, and they both became ashamed of them. They finally agreed that either should say anything he pleased about the other, and it should not be resented as an offense; and from that time on the campaign progressed without any special display of ill temper.

On election night the two candidates, who lived in the same town, were receiving the returns together, and the contest was uncomfortably close. A distant precinct in which one of the candidates confidently expected a large majority was finally reported with a majority against him. The disappointed candidate expressed great surprise, to which the other candidate answered that either was free to say anything about the other without offense and added that, under that authority, he had gone up into the district and taken the liberty of saying that his opponent had retired from the contest, and therefore the vote of the district was changed, and the "declined" candidate was thus defeated.

I think I had better "decline" Chase.

Putting Damages in Perspective.

That reminds me of a wooden-legged amateur who happened to be with a Virginia skirmishing party when a shell burst near him, smashing his artificial limb to bits and sending a piece of iron through the calf of a soldier near him. The soldier "grinned and bore it" like a man, while the amateur was loud and emphatic in his lamentation. Being rebuked by the wounded soldier, he replied: "Oh, yes; it's all well enough for you to bear it. Your leg didn't cost you anything and will heal up; but I paid two hundred dollars for mine!"

A Good Response to Someone Who Asks Your Opinion about Something You Don't Particularly Like.

You remind me of a young lawyer in Sangamon County who had hung out his shingle for a long time without having a client. At last he got one, but feeling very anxious not to lose his first case, he thought he would go down and state it to the justice who was to try it and ascertain in advance what he thought of it. So he went down one Sunday evening and stated it for all it was worth and concluded by asking the justice how he would probably decide it. "As you state the case," replied the justice, "I should be obliged to decide against you. But you had better bring the case. Probably the other side will make so much worse a showing that I shall have to decide the case in your favor."

A Good Story to Tell When Defending a Hard-Working Subordinate.

Out in my state of Illinois there was a man nominated for sheriff of the county. He was a good man for the office, brave, determined, and honest, but not much of an orator. In fact, he couldn't talk at all; he couldn't make a speech to save his life.

His friends knew he was a man who would preserve the peace of the county and perform the duties devolving upon him all right, but the people of the county didn't know it. They wanted him to come out boldly on the platform at political meetings and state his convictions and principles. They had been used to speeches from candidates and were somewhat suspicious of a man who was afraid to open his mouth.

At last the candidate consented to make a speech, and his friends were delighted. The candidate was on hand, and, when he was called upon, advanced to the front and faced the crowd. There was a glitter in his eye that wasn't pleasing, and the way he walked out to the front of the stand showed that he knew just what he wanted to say.

"Feller Citizens," was his beginning, the words spoken quietly, "I'm not a speakin' man; I ain't no orator, an' I never stood up before a lot of people in my life before; I'm not goin' to make no speech 'cept to say that I can lick any man in the crowd!"
[Lincoln told this in defense of General Grant.]

When People Ask You for Something You Don't Have.

I feel very much in the position of the man who was attacked by a robber demanding his money when he answered: "My dear fellow, I have no money, but if you will go with me to the light, I will give you my note."

A Good Reply When Nobody Likes Your Idea.

This reminds me of the story of the man who had been away from home, and when he was coming back was met by one of his farmhands who greeted him after this fashion: "Master, the little pigs are dead, and the old sow's dead, too, but I didn't like to tell you all at once."

This reminds me of a story of a sea captain who ran his vessel on a rock and knocked a hole in her bottom. He set his men to pumping, and he went to pray before a figure of the Virgin in the bow of the ship. The leak gained on them. It looked at last as if the vessel would go down with all on board. The captain at length, in a fit of rage at not having his prayers answered, seized the figure of the Virgin and threw it overboard. Suddenly, the leak stopped, the water was pumped out, and the vessel got safely into port. When docked for repairs, the statue of the Virgin Mary was found stuck head foremost in the hole.

Illustrating Neutrality and Sympathy for Both Sides.

I am reminded of a preacher named Josh who was once trying to enlighten old Joe about the importance of religion and the danger of the future.

"There are two roads before you, Joe," said Josh. "Be careful which one you take. One path is narrow and leads straight to destruction; but broad is the other path that leads right to damnation."

Old Joe opened his eyes with fright, and, under the spell of the awful danger before him, exclaimed: "Josh, take which road you please; I shall go through the woods."

I can best illustrate my position in regard to your St. Louis quarrel by telling a story. A man in Illinois had a watermelon patch on which he hoped to make money enough to carry him through the year. A big hog broke through the log fence nearly every night, and the melons were gradually disappearing. At length the farmer told his son John to get out the guns, and they would promptly dispose of the disturber of their melon patch. They followed the tracks to a neighboring creek where they disappeared. They discovered them on the opposite bank and waded through. They kept on the trail a couple of hundred yards when the tracks again went into the creek but promptly turned up on the other side. Once more the hunters buffeted the mud and water and again struck the lead and pushed on a few furlongs when the tracks made another drive into the creek. Out of breath and patience, the farmer said: "John, you cross over and go up on that side and I'll keep on this side, for I believe the old fellow is on both sides."

Gentlemen, that is just where I stand in regard to your controversies in St. Louis. I am on both sides.

A Good Reply When Someone Asks You How You Like Your Job.

Well, you have heard the story, haven't you, about the man as he was ridden out of town on a rail, tarred and feathered? Somebody asked him how he liked it, and his reply was if it was not for the honor of the thing, he would much rather walk.

[Lincoln's reply when asked how he liked being president of the United States.]

A Good Reply to a Self-Proclaimed Expert.

Question: How many legs will a sheep have if you call the tail a leg?
Answer: Five.
Reply: No, because calling a tail a leg doesn't make it one.
[And calling yourself a leader doesn't make you one.]

PART
III

Lincoln's Colloquialisms

It is an old maxim and a very sound one that he that dances should always pay the fiddler. Now, sir, in the present case, if any gentlemen whose money is a burden to them, choose to lead off a dance, I am decidedly opposed to the people's money being used to pay the fiddler.

He may yet be taught to sing a different song.

I was fixed "firm as the surge repelling rock" in my resolution.

We all feel that we know that a blast of wind would extinguish the flame of the candle...How do we know it?...We know it because we have seen through all our lives that a blast of wind extinguishes the flame of a candle whenever it is thrown fully upon it.

Why build the cage if they expect to catch no birds?

They are most distressingly affected in their heels *with a species of* "running itch."

❦

Intensity *of thought...will sometimes wear the sweetest idea threadbare and turn it to the bitterness of death.*

❦

It grins out like a copper dollar.

❦

In getting Baker the nomination, I shall be "fixed" a good deal like a fellow who is made groomsman to the man what has cut him out and is marrying his own dear "gal."

❦

An evil *tree cannot bring forth* good *fruit.*

❦

This opinion of Mr. Jefferson, in one branch at least, is, in the hands of Mr. Polk, like McFingal's gun: "Bears wide and kicks the owner over."

❦

Let everyone play the part he can play best—some speak, some sing, and all holler.

❦

A fellow once advertised that he had made a discovery by which he could make a new man out of an old one and have enough of the stuff left to make a little yellow dog.

Like a horde of hungry ticks, you have stuck to the tail of the Hermitage lion to the end of his life....

Mr. Speaker, old horses and military coat-tails, or tails of any sort, are not figures of speech, such as I would be the first to introduce into discussions here; but as the gentleman from Georgia has thought fit to introduce them, he and you are welcome to all you have made, or can make, by them. If you have any more old horses, trot them out; any more tails, just cock them and come at us.

It is like the pair of pantaloons the Yankee peddler offered for sale—"large enough for any man, small enough for any boy."

After an angry and dangerous controversy, the parties made friends by dividing the bone of contention....It is as if two starving men had divided their only loaf; the one had hastily swallowed his half and then grabbed the other half just as he was putting it to his mouth!

Some poet has said: "Fools rush in where angels fear to tread." At the hazard of being thought one of the fools of this quotation, I meet that argument—I rush in, I take that bull by the horns.

This is as plain as the adding up of the weights of three small hogs.

He is in the cat's paw. By much dragging of chestnuts from the fire for others to eat, his claws are burnt off to the gristle, and he is thrown aside as unfit for further use.

Like a rejected lover making merry at the wedding of his rival...

Acting on this as a precedent, I say, "Here's your old 'chalked hat.' I wish you would take it and send me a new one case I shall want to use it the first of March."

They [authors of the Declaration of Independence] knew the proneness of prosperity to breed tyrants, and they meant when such should reappear in this fair land and commence their vocation, they should find left for them at least one hard nut to crack.

The plainest print cannot be read through a gold eagle.

It should be throttled and killed as hastily and as heartily as a rabid dog.

These things look like the cautious patting and petting a spirited horse, preparatory to mounting him, when it is dreaded that he may give the rider a fall.

A living dog is better than a dead lion.

It is to be dished up in as many varieties as a French cook can produce soups from potatoes.

I planted myself upon the truth, and the truth only, so far as I knew it or could be brought to know it.

A specious and fantastic arrangement of words by which a man can prove a horse chestnut to be a chestnut horse.

Douglas and I, for the first time this canvass, crossed swords here yesterday. The fire flew some, and I am glad to know I am yet alive.

I have no way of making an argument up into the consistency of a corn cob and stopping his (Stephen A. Douglas) mouth with it.

Has it got down as thin as the homeopathic soup that was made by boiling the shadow of a pigeon that had starved to death?

The last tip of the last joint of the old serpent's tail was just drawing out of view.

It would be a great thing, when this trick is attempted upon us, to have the saddle come up on the other horse.

I feel somewhat like the boy in Kentucky who stubbed his toe while running to see his sweetheart. He said he was too big to cry and too badly hurt to laugh.

Like wood for ox-bows, they are merely being soaked in it, preparatory to the bending.

That is cool. A highwayman holds a pistol to my ear and mutters through his teeth, "Stand and deliver or I shall kill you, and then you will be a murderer!"

If that's the plan, they should begin at the foundation and adopt the well-known "Georgia costume" of a shirt-collar and pair of spurs!

I think that one of the causes of these repeated failures is that our best and greatest men have greatly underestimated the size of this question. They have constantly brought forward small cures for great sores—plasters too small to cover the wound.

The store winked out.

On that point hold firm—as with a chain of steel.

As they say in the hayfield, he requires a good man to 'rake after him.' If such men were in command there would be a movement at the front. I can find men enough who can rake after, but the men with long arms and broad shoulders who swing a scythe in long sweeps, cutting a swath ten feet wide, are much more difficult to find.

I don't amount to pig tracks in the War Department.

I would be as powerless as a block of buck-eye wood.

The advocates of that theory always remind me of the fellow who contended that the proper place for the big kettle was inside of the little one.

Small potatoes and few in a hill.

Yes, it is a heavy hog to hold.

Every foul bird comes abroad, and every dirty reptile rises up.

*A short and feeble existence, as an animal
with a thorn in its vitals.*

*As likely to capture the man in the moon as
any part of Lee's army.*

We won't jump that ditch till we come to it.

*A jury too frequently has at least one
member more ready to hang the panel
than the traitor.*

A good Irish bull is medicine for the blues.

*Now, my man, go away! I cannot attend to
all these details. I could as easily bail out
the Potomac with a spoon.*

*You are green, it is true; but they are green,
also; you are all green alike.*

Well, I will be better now, I guess, for I have got down to the raisins.

The Republican Party should not be a mere sucked egg, all shell and no meat, the principle all sucked out.

That thunderbolt will keep.

Bricks in his pocket will be better than bricks in his hat.

It's a good rule never to send a mouse to catch a skunk or a pollywog to tackle a whale.

You must know that major generalships in the Regular Army are not as plenty as blackberries.

Assuming this, it is for you a question of legs. Put in all the speed you can.

Shields' division has got so terribly out of shape, out at elbows, and out at toes, that it will require a long time to get it in again.

He's (McClellan) got the slows.

What would you do in my position? Would you drop the war where it is? Or, would you prosecute it in future, with elder-stalk squirts, charged with rose water?

The bottom is out of the tub! The bottom is out of the tub!

Calling McClellan to power again is a good deal like curing the bite with the hair of the dog.

If the battle had gone against us, poor McClellan and I, too, would be in a bad row of stumps.

It's like trying to ride a balky horse. You coax, and cheer, and spur, and lay on the whip, but you don't get ahead an inch—there you stick!

I do not want to issue a document that the whole world will see must necessarily be inoperative, like the Pope's bull against the comet!

This is not the Army of the Potomac. This is General McClellan's bodyguard.

I shall have to cut this knot.

If I had said yes and had appointed the judge, I should—as he would have done his duty—have simply touched a match to a barrel of gunpowder. You have heard of sitting on a volcano. We are sitting upon two; one is blazing away already, and the other will blaze away the moment we scrape a little loose dirt from the top of the crater. Better let the dirt alone—at least for the present. One rebellion at a time is about as much as we can conveniently handle.

Let 'em root!

We are like whalers who have been on a long chase. We have at last got the harpoon into the monster, but we must now look how we steer, or with one flop of his tail he will send us all into eternity.

If I can only keep my end of the animal pointed in the right direction, I will yet get him through this infernal jungle and get my end of him and his tail placed in their proper relative positions.

Ready are we all to cry out—and ascribe motives—when our own toes are pinched.

The army dwindles on the march like a shovelfull of fleas pitched from one place to another.

*Her business would be to guard a particu-
lar harbor as a bulldog guards his
master's door.*

*In one word, I would not take any risk of
being entangled upon the river, like an ox
jumped half over a fence and liable to be
torn by dogs, front and rear, without a fair
chance to gore one way or kick the other.*

*If the head of Lee's army is at Martinsburg
and the tail of it on the Plank Road
between Fredericksburg and
Chancellorsville, the animal must be very
slim somewhere. Could you not break him?*

*He (Meade) will fight well on his
own dunghill.*

*Our army held the war in the hollow of
their hand, and they would not close it. We
had gone through all the labor of tilling
and planting an enormous crop, and when
it was ripe we did not harvest it.*

Do you know, General (Meade), what your attitude toward Lee after the Battle of Gettysburg reminded me of?...I'll be hanged if I could think of anything but an old woman trying to shoo her geese across a creek.

We will condemn him as they used to sell hogs in Indiana, as they run.

We are contending with an enemy who, as I understand, drives every able-bodied man he can reach into his ranks, very much as a butcher drives bullocks into a slaughter pen.

Nor must Uncle Sam's web feet be forgotten. At all the watery margins they have been present.

I understand the main body of the enemy is very near you, so near that you could "board at home," so to speak, and menace or attack him any day.

He (General Rosecrans) is confused and stunned like a duck hit on the head.

I suppose he (Salmon P. Chase) will, like the bluebottle fly, lay his eggs in every rotten spot he can find.

It would be a perpetual flea hunt.

By jings!

Lamon, that speech (Gettysburg Address) won't scour. It is a flat failure, and the people are disappointed.

A senator or representative out of business is a sort of lame duck. He has to be provided for.

This powder has been shot before.

I learned a great many years ago that in a fight between man and wife, a third party should never get between the woman's skillet and the man's ax helve.

That fixes him out.

Well, I have got that job husked out. Now, I guess I will go over to the War Department before I go to bed and see if there is any news.

I have a pumpkin at each end of my bag.

They are like two dogs that get less eager to fight the nearer they come to each other.

I do not perceive anything necessarily inconsistent with the practice of detectives and others, engaged in the business of "rascal-catching."

I knew that another beehive was kicked over.

By general law life and limb must be protected; yet often a limb must be amputated to save a life; but a life is never wisely given to save a limb.

He (Halleck) broke down—nerve and pluck all gone—and has ever since evaded all possible responsibility—little more since that than a first-rate clerk.

Those not skinning can hold a leg.

Grant is like the man that climbed the pole and then pulled the pole up after him.

Grant has gone to the Wilderness, crawled in, drawn up the ladder, and pulled in the hole after him, and I guess we'll have to wait till he comes out before we know just what he's up to.

No man knows so well where the shoe pinches as he who wears it.

The only thing to do is to keep pegging away.

Let 'em wriggle.

Hold on with a bulldog grip and chew and choke as much as possible.

He [Horace Greeley] is like an old shoe— good for nothing now, whatever he has been. In early life, and with few mechanics and but little means in the West, we used to make our shoes last a great while with much mending, and sometimes, when far gone, we found the leather so rotten the stitches would not hold. Greeley is so rotten that nothing can be done with him. He is not truthful; the stitches all tear out.

In politics, every man must skin his own skunk.

I'll be dumped on the right side of that stream.

There are too many pigs for the teats.

I shall be very "shut pan" about this matter.

I would rather have swallowed my buckhorn chair than to have nominated Chase 'Chief Justice of the Supreme Court'.

The most interesting news we now have is from Sherman. We all know where he went in, but I can't tell where he will come out.

Did you see him take off his overcoat, Grant? Well, didn't you think it was the biggest shuck and the smallest nubbin you ever did see?

BIBLIOGRAPHY

Basler, Roy P., editor, 1953. *The Collected Works of Abraham Lincoln*. Rutgers Univ. Press, 8 vols., New Jersey. (CW)

Dennett, Tyler, editor, 1939. *The Diaries and Letters of John Hay*. Dodd, Mead & Company Inc., New York.

Hertz, Emmanuel, 1939. *Lincoln Talks, a Biography in Anecdote*. Halcyon House, New York.

Lamon, Ward H., 1895. *Recollections of Abraham Lincoln: 1847-1865*. A.C. McClurg and Company, Chicago.

McClure, Alexander K., 1901. *Abe Lincoln's Yarns and Stories*. Winston, Philadelphia.

Randall, J.G., 1952. *Lincoln the President*, Vol. 2. Dodd, Mead & Company, New York.

Bibliography

Reports of the Committee on the Conduct of the War, 1863, Vol. 2, p. 6. Washington, D.C.

Sandburg, Carl, 1936-1939. *Abraham Lincoln, the War Years.* Harcourt, Brace & World, Inc., New York.

Thomas, Benjamin P., 1952. *Abraham Lincoln.* Alfred A. Knopf, Inc., New York.

Welles, Gideon, 1911. *The Diary of Gideon Welles,* Houghton Mifflin Co., Boston.

Williams, T. Harry, 1952. *Lincoln and His Generals.* Alfred A. Knopf, Inc., New York.

Zall, P. M., 1982. *Abe Lincoln Laughing.* University of California Press, Berkeley.

NOTES

INTRODUCTION

Story about woman on horseback from Zall, p. 259; "Abraham is joking" from Zall, p. 151; Schurz quote from Schurz, p. 253; "I believe I have the popular reputation of being a story-teller" from Hertz, pp. 638-639; "shoot it out of a popgun" from Zall, p. 9; Zall, p. 5; Thurlow Weed comment from Thomas, p. 485; "Lincoln to Weed" from CW, Vol. 6, p. 514; "a good laugh" from Sandburg, Vol. 3, p. 305; "cheer up people in this hard world," from Zall, p. 6; "little pigs are dead" story from Zall, p. 157; "They say I tell a great many stories," from Hertz, p. 630; "Virgin Mary" story from Hertz, pp. 221-222; Peters and Austin, pp. 278, 281; "an old shoe" from Welles, Vol. 2, p. 112; "bluebottle fly" from Dennett, p. 110; "I don't amount to pig tracks" from Sandburg, Vol. 2, p. 305; "fight well on his own dunghill" from Williams, p. 260; "old woman trying to shoo her geese across a creek" from Sandburg, Vol. 2, p. 436; "confused and

stunned like a duck hit on the head" from
Dennett, p. 106; "McClellan's bodyguard" from
Sandburg, Vol. 1, p. 595; "bad row of stumps"
from Sandburg, Vol. 1, p. 552; "those not skinning can hold a leg" from Dennett, p. 179.

Part I—Lincoln Stories for General Leadership

COMPASSION

"Unbeknownst-like" story from Hertz, pp. 369-
370.

CONSISTENCY

"Not best to swap horses when crossing
streams" from CW, Vol. 7, p. 384; "fought himself *out* of his own coat, and *into* that of the
other's" from CW, Vol. 3, p. 375.

DECISIVENESS

"I must have it to quiet myself" from Zall, p.
148; "lion and the woodman's daughter" from
Hertz, p. 262; "Tightrope walker" from Hertz,
p. 263; "don't want no one sneakin' 'round tryin'
to find out how I do it" from McClure, pp. 342-
343; "who commenced this fuss?" from Zall, p.
91.

FLEXIBILITY

"If it's good for him he has got it, but if it isn't good for him he hasn't" from Zall, p. 81; "I shot at it so as to hit it if it was a deer and miss it if a calf" from Zall, p. 113.

GET TO THE CORE; DON'T WASTE TIME

"Old Bill Sikes' dog" from Hertz, pp. 318-319; "It comes out of the same side of the log" from Zall, pp. 59-60; "I've lost my apple overboard!" from Zall, p. 36; "every time the whistle blew the boat had to stop" from Zall, p. 118; "a little more light and a little less noise!" from Zall, pp. 65-66; "Lazy preacher" from Zall, pp. 98-99; "I believe in punishment after death" from Lamon, pp. 220-221; "Damn the details!" from Zall, p. 65.

HONESTY AND INTEGRITY

"I take nothing but money" from Zall, p. 88.

HUMAN NATURE

"Two bulldogs separated by a fence" from Hertz, p. 357.

INNOVATION

"Slavery is a wart on the government" from Hertz, pp. 329-330; "make a noise like a turnip" from Hertz, pp. 607-608; "the swearing had to be done then or not at all" from Zall, p. 73.

MOTIVATION
"Presidential chin-fly" from Hertz, p. 226.

PATIENCE—AVOID RASHNESS
"I embraced her before I popped the question" from Hertz, pp. 225-226; "The careless barber" from Zall, p. 34; "The fining judge" from Hertz, p. 491; "Fourth of July celebration" from Hertz, pp. 569-571.

PERSISTENCE
"I'll keep on sweeping as long as the broom lasts" from Sandburg, Vol. 3, p. 383; "no other way but to plow around it" from Zall, p. 74; "Two men about to fight" from McClure, pp. 38-39; " My dog is always mad" from Zall, p. 76.

VISION
"How to get the boy out" from Hertz, p. 554; "I will make a fizzle anyhow" from Hertz, p. 568-569; "in no place up to his ankles" from Zall, pp. 105-106; "if I should happen to get well—that old grudge stands!" from Zall, pp. 94-95; "You've been firing at a louse on your eyebrow" from Hertz, p. 121; "additional tail about him until its weight broke him down" from Zall, p. 86; "Dashing Jack got the apple" from Zall, pp. 130-131.

Part II—Lincoln Stories for Practical Leadership Situations

"There won't be any fun till I get there" from Lamon, p. 132; "anxious to have the hanging postponed" from Hertz, p. 295; "I have got down to the raisins" from McClure, pp. 36-37; "it's nothing but a noise" from Zall, p. 47; "I just wanted to see her spread herself" from Hertz, pp. 641-642; "what in the infernals are you passing for when people are shouting 'Hello'?" from Hertz, p. 607; "If you are going to get on, I will get off" from Hertz, p. 459; "There's too many dogs in here now!" from Sandburg, Vol. 3, p. 333; "chickens crossed their legs ready to be tied," from Hertz, pp. 279-280; "Heroic soldiers from the crusades," from Hertz, p. 236; "a yard full of old bulls" from Hertz, pp. 434-435; "every jackass wants an office" from Zall, pp. 24-25; "none of them are any great shakes" from Zall, p. 58; "Boy at ship's launching" from Lamon, pp. 139-140; "Now, Ma, I can surely run out and play" from Sandburg, Vol. 3, p. 322; "I guess I'll float a little farther" from Zall, p. 28; "carried him out to die in the gutter" from McClure, pp. 73-74; "It decorates the ruin it makes" from Hertz, p. 586; "feller takes in swaring for a livin!" from Zall, p. 145; "he hoped the court would be lenient to him because he was a poor orphan!" from Hertz, p. 266; "Give me back that pistol; you have no right to my property" from Hertz, p. 338; "I only wants what joins mine" from Zall, p. 144; "Somebody loses; but I don't know as yet who it is" from Hertz, pp. 312-313; "always a little puzzled when it came to mending a broken leg" from Zall, p. 48; "Squirrel and the hollow tree" from Hertz, pp. 362-364; "I have got you reduced to a portable shape, so I'll put you in my pocket" from Lamon, p. 37; "let somebody run that knows how" from Zall, p. 121; "Let 'em root!" from Zall, p. 49; "About a foot!" from Zall, p. 97; "allowed for the durn'd thing crawling" from Hertz, pp. 124-125; "sleep with the supervisor of this town" from Hertz, p. 269; "I think I had better decline Chase" from Hertz, pp. 227-228; "Your leg didn't cost you anything" from Hertz, p. 320; "I shall have to decide the case in your favor" from Zall, p. 95; "I can lick any man in the crowd!" from McClure, p. 348; "if you will go with me to the light, I will give you my note" from Zall, p. 17; "I didn't like to tell you all at once" from Zall, p. 157; "Virgin Mary was found stuck head foremost in the hole" from Hertz, pp. 221-222; "I shall go through the woods" from McClure, pp. 28-29; "I believe the old fellow is on both sides" from Hertz, pp. 266-267; if it was not for the honor of the thing, he would much rather walk" from Zall, p. 143; "calling a tail a leg doesn't make it one" from Hertz, p. 328.

Part III—Lincoln's Colloquialisms

CW, Vol. 1, p. 64 (January 11, 1837);
CW, Vol. 1, p. 104 (October 18, 1837);
CW, Vol. 1, p. 118 (April 1, 1838);
CW, Vol. 1, p. 165 (December 26, 1839);
CW, Vol. 1, p. 169 (December 26, 1839);
CW, Vol. 1, p. 177 (December 26, 1839):
CW, Vol. 1, p. 265 (January 3, 1842);
CW, Vol. 1, p. 295 (August 27, 1842);
CW, Vol. 1, p. 319 (March 24, 1843);
CW, Vol. 1, p. 347 (October 3, 1845);
CW, Vol. 1, p. 485 (June 20, 1848);
CW, Vol. 1, p. 491 (June 22, 1848);
CW, Vol. 1, p. 508 (July 27, 1848);
CW, Vol. 1, p. 508 (July 27, 1848);
CW, Vol. 1, pp. 508-509 (July 27, 1848);
CW, Vol. 2, p. 3 (September 12, 1848);
CW, Vol. 2, p. 262 (October 16, 1854);
CW, Vol. 2, p. 265 (October 16, 1854);
CW, Vol. 2, p. 374 (September 8, 1856);
CW, Vol. 2, p. 384 (December 10, 1856);
CW, Vol. 2, p. 384 (December 10, 1856);
CW, Vol. 2, p. 330 (December 13, 1856);
CW, Vol. 2, p. 406 (June 26, 1857);

CW, Vol. 2, p. 409 (June 26, 1857);

CW, Vol. 2, p. 450 (May 18, 1858);

CW, Vol. 2, p. 465 (June 16, 1858);

CW, Vol. 2, p. 467 (June 16, 1858);

CW, Vol. 2, p. 507 (July 17, 1858);

CW, Vol. 2, p. 512 (July 17, 1858);

CW, Vol. 3, p. 16 (August 21, 1858);

CW, Vol. 3, p. 37 (August 22, 1858);

CW, Vol. 3, p. 118 (September 16, 1858);

CW, Vol. 3, p. 279 (October 13, 1858);

CW, Vol. 3, p. 306 (October 15, 1858);

CW, Vol. 3, p. 330 (October 20, 1858);

Zall, p. 22 (November 1858);

CW, Vol. 3, p. 431 (September 16-17, 1859);

CW, Vol. 3, p. 547 (February 27, 1860);

CW, Vol. 4, p. 12 (March 5, 1860);

CW, Vol. 4, p. 15 (March 6, 1860);

CW, Vol. 4, p. 65 (June 1860);

CW, Vol. 4, p. 151 (December 13, 1860);

Sandburg, *The War Years*, Vol. 2, p. 299 (1861-1864);

Sandburg, *The War Years*, Vol. 2, p. 305 (1861-1864);

Sandburg, *The War Years*, Vol. 1, pp. 12-13 (1861-1864);

Zall, pp. 55-56 (1861-1864);

Sandburg, *The War Years*, Vol. 3, p. 321 (1861-1864);

Sandburg, *The War Years*, Vol. 3, p. 336 (1861-1864);

Sandburg, *The War Years*, Vol. 3, p. 321 (1861-1864);

Sandburg, *The War Years*, Vol. 3, p. 321 (1861-1864);

Sandburg, *The War Years*, Vol. 3, p. 321 (1861-1864);

Sandburg, *The War Years*, Vol. 1, p. 34 (1861-1864);

Sandburg, *The War Years*, Vol. 3, p. 321 (1861-1864);

Sandburg, *The War Years*, Vol. 2, p. 313 (1861-1864);

Diary of John Hay, pp. 324-325 (1861);

Reports of the Committee on the Conduct of the War, 1863, Vol. 2, p. 36;

Sandburg, *The War Years*, Vol. 2, p. 241 (1861);

Sandburg, *The War Years*, p. 306 (July 1861);

Sandburg, *The War Years*, Vol. 1, pp. 356-357 (September 1861); Zall, p. 107 (1862);

Sandburg, *The War Years*, Vol. 1, p. 489 (1862);

CW, Vol. 5, p. 186 (April 10, 1862);

CW, Vol. 5, p. 246 (May 28, 1862);

CW, Vol. 5, p. 272 (June 15, 1862);

Sandburg, *The War Years*, Vol. 1, p. 491 (June 1862);

CW, Vol. 5, p. 346 (July 28, 1862);

Sandburg, *The War Years*, Vol. 1, p. 534 (August 1862);

Sandburg, *The War Years*, Vol. 1, p. 544 (August 1862);

Sandburg, *The War Years*, Vol. 1, p. 552
(September 1862);
Sandburg, *The War Years*, Vol. 1, p. 554.
(September 1862);
CW, Vol. 5, p. 420 (September 13, 1862);
Sandburg, *The War Years*, Vol. 1, p. 595
(October 1862);
Sandburg, *The War Years*, Vol. 1, p. 659
(December 1862);
Sandburg, *The War Years*, Vol. 2, p. 368 (1863);
Zall, p. 49. (1863);
Sandburg, *The War Years*, Vol. 2, p. 21
(January 1863);
Sandburg, *The War Years*, Vol. 2, p. 176
(February 1863);
CW, Vol. 6, p. 139 (March 17, 1863);
Diary of John Hay, p. 53 (March-May 1863);
CW, Vol. 6, p. 163 (April 4, 1863);
CW, Vol. 6, p. 249 (June 5, 1863);
CW, Vol. 6, p. 273 (June 14, 1863);
Williams, p. 260 (June 28, 1863);
Diary of John Hay, p. 69 (July 19, 1863);
Diary of John Hay, p. 69 (July 19, 1863);
CW, Vol. 6, p. 370 (August 7, 1863);
CW, Vol. 6, p. 409 (August 26, 1863);
Sandburg, *The War Years*, Vol. 2, p. 436
(October 1863);
CW, Vol. 6, p. 498 (October 4, 1863);

Diary of John Hay, p. 106 (October 24, 1863);
Diary of John Hay, p. 110 (October 29, 1863);
Sandburg, *The War Years*, Vol. 3, p. 349 (November 1863);
Sandburg, *The War Years*, Vol. 3, p. 369 (November 1863);
Lamon, p. 171. (November 19, 1863);
Sandburg, *The War Years*, Vol. 3, p. 454 (1864);
Hertz, pp. 296-297 (1864);
Hertz, p. 292 (1864);
Thomas, p. 498 (1864);
Sandburg, *The War Years*, Vol. 3, p. 415. (1864);
J.G. Randall, *Lincoln the President*, Vol. 2, p. 247-248 (February 1864);
Sandburg, *The War Years*, Vol. 3, pp. 331-332 (February 1864); CW, Vol. 7, p. 195 (February 20, 1864);
Sandburg, *The War Years*, Vol. 3, p. 35 (March 1864);
CW, Vol. 7, p. 281 (April 4, 1864);
Diary of John Hay, p. 176 (April 28, 1864);
Dennett, p. 179 (April 30, 1864);
Zall, p. 44 (May 16, 1864);
Sandburg, *The War Years*, Vol. 3, p. 43 (May 1864);
Sandburg, *The War Years*, Vol. 3, p. 111 (June 1864);
Sandburg, *The War Years*, Vol. 3, pp. 408-409 (June 1864);

Diary of John Hay, p. 203 (July 1, 1864);
CW, Vol. 7, p. 499 (August 17, 1864);
Diary of Gideon Welles, Vol. 2, p. 112 (August 19, 1864);
Lamon, p. 142 (September 1864);
Lamon, p. 206 (November 1864);
McClure, p. 90 (December 1864);
Sandburg, *The War Years*, Vol. 3, p. 596 (December 1864);
Welles, *Diary*, Vol. 2, p. 196.;
CW, Vol. 8, p. 154 (December 6, 1864);
Sandburg, *The War Years*, Vol. 4, p. 45 (1864-1865).

INDEX

W
Weed, Thurlow, xvii

Y
Yazoo River, 15

ABOUT THE AUTHOR

Donald T. Phillips is the author of *Lincoln on Leadership* (Warner Books), which elucidates Abraham Lincoln's leadership style and how it can be applied in today's complex society. A bestseller and currently in its 9th printing, *Lincoln on Leadership* has been published in seven different languages. Mr. Phillips is also the coauthor of On the Brink (Summit), an autobiographical account of the life of Norman Brinker. He is widely recognized in the field of leadership and speaks frequently around the country to various corporations, government groups and professional organizations. He lives in Fairview, Texas with his wife and three children.